You with the Stars in Your Eyes

A little girl's glimpse at Cosmic Consciousness

Dr. Deepak Chopra

Illustrated by Dave Zaboski

HAY HOUSE, INC.
Carlsbad, California • New York City
London • Sydney • Johannesburg
Vancouver • Hong Kong • New Delhi

Published and distributed in the United States by: Hay House, Inc.: www.hayhouse.com
Published and distributed in Australia by: Hay House Australia Pty. Ltd.: www.hayhouse.com.au
Published and distributed in the United Kingdom by: Hay House UK, Ltd.: www.hayhouse.co.uk
Published and distributed in the Republic of South Africa by: Hay House SA (Pty), Ltd.: www.hayhouse.co.za
Distributed in Canada by: Raincoast: www.raincoast.com
Published in India by: Hay House Publishers India: www.hayhouse.co.in

Design: Dave Zaboski

Library of Congress Control Number: 2009927765

ISBN: 978-1-4019-2711-0

13 12 11 10   4 3 2 1
1st edition, January 2010

Printed in Shenzhen, China, in August 2009 by Bookplus International Ltd

Files submitted to printer: August 19, 2009

This book is dedicated to all the children in the world.

If we could see through their eyes, the world would be healed.

"Twinkle twinkle, little star,
How I wonder who you are,

Up above the world so high,
Like a diamond in the sky . . ."

Tara sang as she walked with her grandfather on a wide flat beach under a canopy of stars. She was five and a half years old, an age when the world is very much alive.

The moon was peeking curiously over the horizon; the waves crept in to tickle Tara's toes and listen.

"I love you very much,"
Tara's grandfather said to her.

"More than all the
stars in the sky,"
he said, spreading
his arms wide.

"Hmm," mused Tara's grandfather. Meanwhile, all kinds of complicated grown-up thoughts jumbled in his head.

"Why?" *Now that **is** a good question,* he thought.

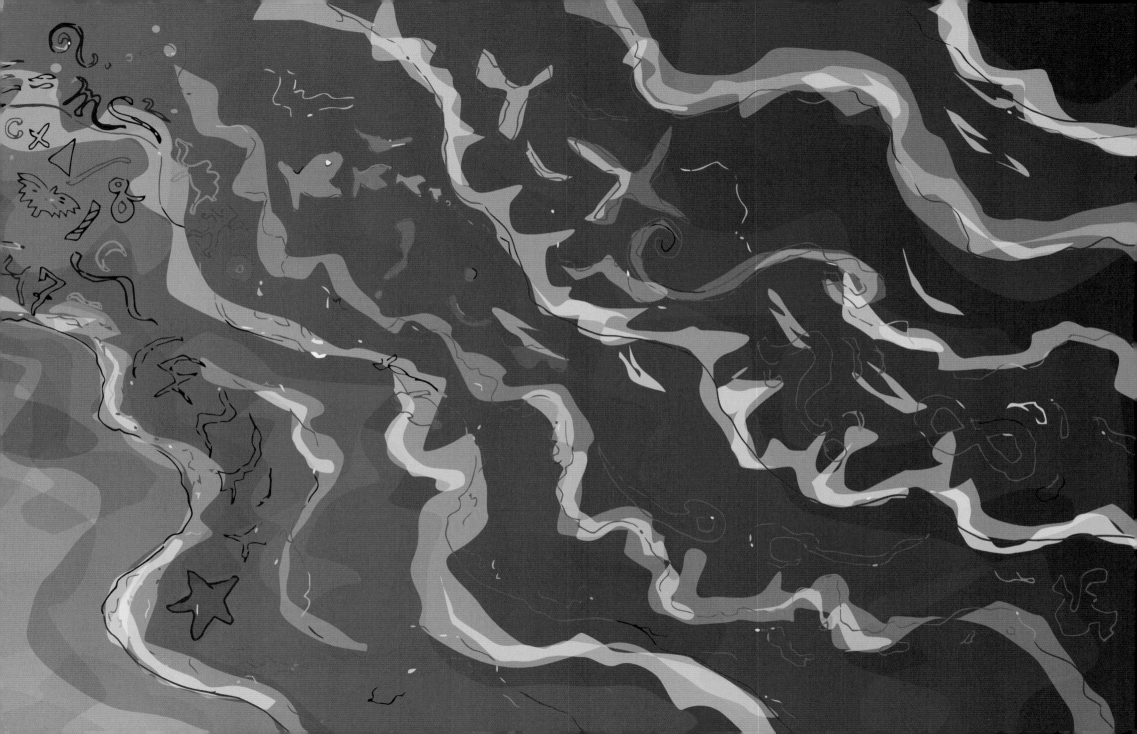

The Moon, who loved to talk of love, had risen and was now strolling along with them in all her finery.

Tara asked, "How? How did I come from the stars?"

"The way you all do, little one, carried on a beam of light."

"On a beam of light? How?" asked Tara, happy to be talking with the Moon.

"Our light streams down and makes the wind blow, the grasses grow, and the dew drops glow. Our light gets into all things."

"What about our eyes?" asked Tara. "Who made our eyes?"

"Ah! That's the most important thing!" exclaimed the Moon.

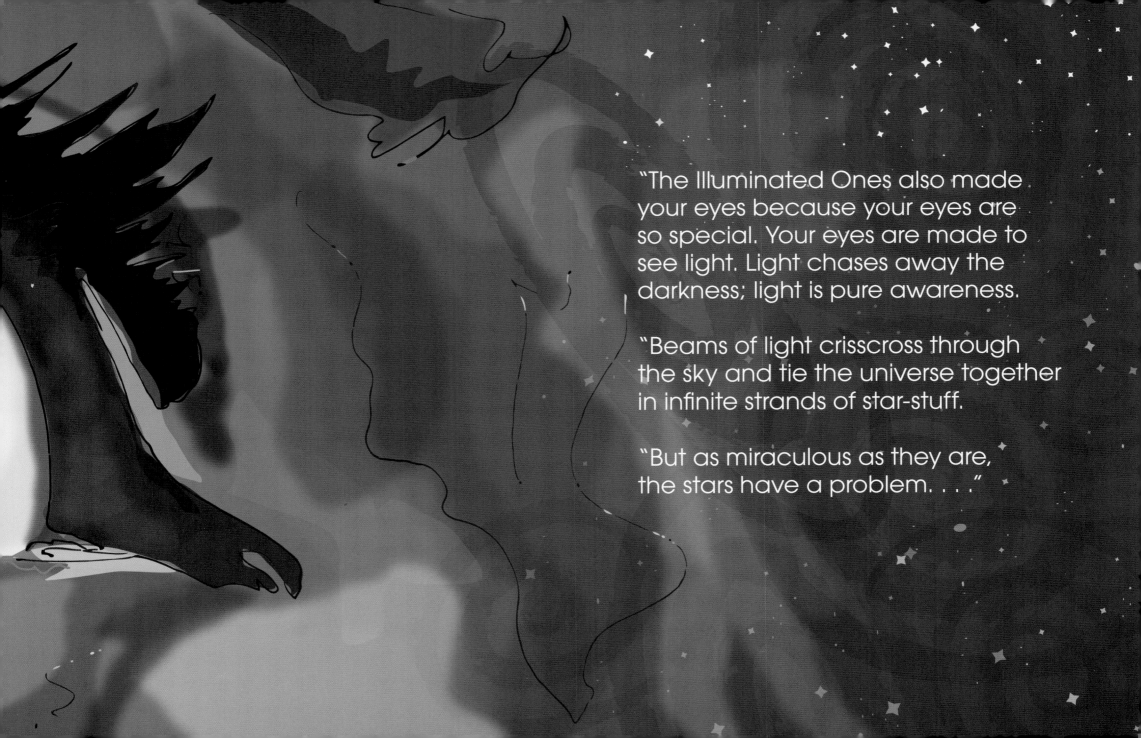

"The Illuminated Ones also made your eyes because your eyes are so special. Your eyes are made to see light. Light chases away the darkness; light is pure awareness.

"Beams of light crisscross through the sky and tie the universe together in infinite strands of star-stuff.

"But as miraculous as they are, the stars have a problem. . . ."

"What's the problem?"
asked Tara's grandfather.

"They have no mirror in space. They cannot see their own beauty. They made your eyes because they need you."

The thought dawned on Tara, "So the stars made my eyes so they could see themselves?"

"Yes, indeed, my dear."
The Moon smiled.
"You all have stars in
your eyes."

"We all have
stars in our eyes!"
Tara liked that
very much.

Tara's grandfather marked the moon and turned to leave the beach, but Tara lingered, her head uplifted, her small feet slowly sinking into the sand. She thought she could hear the waves whispering as they rushed up onto the shore. She began to sing:

"Twinkle twinkle, little star,

Now I know just what I see . . .

I am You, and You are ME!"

Tara ran giggling to her grandfather and tugged on his pants leg. "Look up, Grandpa!" she exclaimed.

"The stars want to see themselves!"

And see themselves they do!
Every time we look up into
their shining faces. . . .

The End

We hope you enjoyed this Hay House book. If you'd like to receive our online catalog featuring additional information on Hay House books and products, or if you'd like to find out more about the Hay Foundation, please contact:

Hay House, Inc.
P.O. Box 5100
Carlsbad, CA 92018-5100

(760) 431-7695 or **(800) 654-5126**
(760) 431-6948 (fax) or **(800) 650-5115 (fax)**
www.hayhouse.com® • **www.hayfoundation.org**

***

Published and distributed in Australia by:

Hay House Australia Pty. Ltd., 18/36 Ralph St., Alexandria NSW 2015 • Phone: 612-9669-4299 • Fax: 612-9669-4144 • www.hayhouse.com.au

Published and distributed in the United Kingdom by:

Hay House UK, Ltd., 292B Kensal Rd., London W10 5BE • Phone: 44-20-8962-1230 • Fax: 44-20-8962-1239 • www.hayhouse.co.uk

Published and distributed in the Republic of South Africa by:

Hay House SA (Pty), Ltd., P.O. Box 990, Witkoppen 2068 • Phone/Fax: 27-11-467-8904 • info@hayhouse.co.za • www.hayhouse.co.za

Published in India by:

Hay House Publishers India, Muskaan Complex, Plot No. 3, B-2, Vasant Kunj, New Delhi 110 070 • Phone: 91-11-4176-1620 • Fax: 91-11-4176-1630 • www.hayhouse.co.in

Distributed in Canada by:

Raincoast, 9050 Shaughnessy St., Vancouver, B.C. V6P 6E5 • Phone: (604) 323-7100 • Fax: (604) 323-2600 • www.raincoast.com

***

Take Your Soul on a Vacation

Visit **HealYourLife.com**® to regroup, recharge, and reconnect with your own magnificence.
Featuring blogs, mind-body-spirit news, and life-changing wisdom from Louise Hay and friends.

Visit **HealYourLife.com** today!